Rise
from the
Blue

RISE
FROM THE
BLUE

BOADE MANDENG

Library of Congress Control Number:		2021904871
ISBN:	Hardcover	978-1-6641-6282-2
	Softcover	978-1-6641-6281-5
	eBook	978-1-6641-6280-8

Print information available on the last page.

Rev. date: 03/09/2021

To order additional copies of this book, contact:
Xlibris
844-714-8691
www.Xlibris.com
Orders@Xlibris.com
822202

CONTENTS

CHAPTER 1

Newest Avenues into Minority Peoples' Politics

NOBOLA: I find it an extremely quisquous thing, sometimes
confusing, to be a person of color while facing and
trying to figure out issues we have to deal with,
especially with recent social developments. It appears
as if many efforts from minorities in general, and
black people in particular, to handle such problems
as police brutality and racial discrimination end up
creating more troubles for these people than they
bring them solutions.

On a quiet Thursday afternoon, John Nobola was on a
routine phone call with his best friend, Isaac Abenda, as he
drove home from work. The day at his business planner office
had been busy, and he would have wanted to talk about this first
thing. However, these days didn't seem ordinary to life as it was

known to most people in Magaville. The news was filled with events that, time after time, brought about constantly changing developments and subsequently left few people indifferent. At the end of his workday, Nobola could not help trying to catch up with Abenda on the hottest topics of the time.

ABENDA: I totally agree with you, John. Protests against injustices to vulnerable franges of the American society have been used by extremists to advance Marxist-like political agendas while other anarchist groups have succeeded to infiltrate waves of demonstrators and turned them into violent hoards. Many black people though, as well as their supporters, while adhering to making the voices of the victims of injustice heard, don't agree on the means because they don't want to be part of criminally and unethically charged activities.

NOBOLA: True. Other aspects of the problem reside in who the common opinion want to blame for issues that face minority groups in general, and blacks in particular. I will point out to cases where black crime results from black perpetrators. In other instances, you have these communities where cries for injustices and discrimination are commonplace, but most leaders there are black or minoritarians themselves; how do you explain or handle that? It is troubling, OMG!

Every social or political discussion these days seemed to always turn into an altercation. Debates filled with confrontational and defiant language was commonplace. Most people, for the sake of civic expression and political participation, had decided to seal allegiance to one or the other of the two American political parties, Republican and Democrat. The first was generally considered to be on the right side of the society while the Dems were mostly known as leftists.

Few on one side wanted to agree with ideas emanating from the other, and this contributed to the polarization of opinions with every debate. In the midst of such social circumstances, Nobola had found an understanding viewpoint partner in his best friend, Abenda. Despite living here in Magaville, a town where most identified as Dems, Nobola was a defender of Republican positions for reasons he was not shy about explaining.

ABENDA: Well, I have another one for you, John: while the mainstream media like to incense all irregular encounters of a black person with police, not to diminish the importance of individual and social trauma that such encounters entice, it is easy to ignore that more murders to blacks by black criminals happen in black neighborhoods at the same time. I tend to think that nobody cares because such incidents are nothing new so they don't make news anymore.

NOBOLA: Exactly, mainstream media want information that captures most, be it fake news don't matter, as long as it gets them the audience that will take care of their bottom line. It doesn't matter to them if the forgotten reality has more social impact. Mainstream media like to feed us with the news that advances their financial and political plans, not necessarily actual reality. Coming from that same realm, you see the frantic activity to make the current pandemic death toll sore to the worst extreme while ignoring that most people by far, who died with COVID-19, were already affected by more debilitating ailments; the purpose thereof is to find a way to prevent a president's reelection, by blaming the deaths on him, non obstante the fact that the public is being lied to in the process. What has happened to ethics in journalism? Do they even care about the people they pretend to report on at all? How about the social well-being of this country?

ABENDA: These are the things that I look into, and I know that it is not hard to take a political stand today in America. Despite what it appears to be, it is not hard to pick between the manipulations from power-hungry politicians and reality; it takes a few fact checks and understanding what is right for the people, not the partisan results. As far as I am concerned, electoral politics can never be the same anymore. The black electorate can no more be considered this locked, singularly opinioned frange of the population, unequivocally committed to the Dems.

NOBOLA: What makes you say that?

ABENDA: I am saying that because Déjà vu, one of their prominent members, has been telling everyone that all blacks must vote for him and other Dems, or else they "ain't black." So much to deal with from someone asking us all to make him our next supreme leader!

ABENDA: Like the Ayatollah, hein! Hahahahaha! You've got to be talking about his understanding of opinion diversity in the black community, right?

NOBOLA: Yes, indeed! His opinion on us black people is that we're not capable of any plurality of thought, and he's been saying it loud and clear; therefore, given that the black electorate is by tradition aligned with the ideals of the party he represents, there's no way getting around.

ABENDA: In other words, anytime a Democrat candidate comes around, he or she can always count on all the votes from the blacks.

What does this suggest? How is such an idea gonna encourage people to think, other than that, no matter what kind of crap a Democrat brings, we must only take without questioning? In the process, black people can live ignorant or deprived of the commonality and diversity of the American dream, and it wouldn't matter. Another implication is that blacks would be kept on the sidelines of the American history, thereby helping to feed a recent narrative presenting this history as full of imperfections. What follows is blacks and other minorities are painted as the victims of those imperfections. Whatever may have happened in the history of the US, as far as I am concerned, whichever side you pick, there have been losers and winners to some degree. Some may have lost less, some won less; the reality is, we are now here in the same boat. We all have this country to save for ourselves and our kids. It's our house to us all, black, white, Hispanic, Arab, or Asian Americans. We choose what to do with our house. But let's keep in mind that a house divided cannot stand.

Efforts for positive progress have been made through the years, which include the promise of Dr. M. L. King's dream of a united America.

NOBOLA: I commend you on that one, Isaac! To stand by the sidelines of the American evolution, perpetually refusing to embrace others because they are of a different color of skin and cultivate the disdain of the republican party because that is not where many blacks go to vote, that is wrong for the future of the US; yet that's the direction most of the Democrat narrative is pushing people to embrace, and that is sinful!

ABENDA: That's true! The demagogue strategy we are now getting from the Democrat's political candidates is to convince voters from black and other minority groups to stick with the Democrat Party and always serve as the party's handy vote insurance. Who cares what we minorities gain back, be it just political peanuts of hardly ever held promises?

NOBOLA: Hey, and there's even more to that, my brother, much more … Now with all the stuff going on these days, it is about time we took a totally new look at the relationship of all so-called minorities, with American politics.

ABENDA: Right, John! The reality about the American society has been going down a new path for a while, and I noticed you have managed ever since to push yourself, and maybe others, to take a big part in the new American conservative, patriotic-oriented revolution.

NOBOLA: Indeed! I noticed a few things that led me to switch political party allegiance, and I went from voting Dem, always, since the beginning, to becoming a Rep four years ago; however, the movement for keeping the American founders' promise for freedom of all in the land of the brave itself has been burgeoning for decades, probably centuries, starting with the birth of this wonderful nation, and constantly evolving for the best. That movement has aimed for no less than a path to potential American perfection throughout the years. How has that been happening? Because of a solid institutional framework of constitutionally inspired laws and rules, and also amazing leaders. That framework, over time, has made America great; unfortunately, greatness has seen flaws at times, and certain groups of politicians, due to partisan and other motives, have had their hands in causing harm to people's quest for happiness.

ABENDA: I can see there a great timeline of causation for your endeavors to shake things into change. It's interesting, and I don't mind getting back with you to discuss this situation again in the near future.

NOBOLA: No problem, brother, and thanks for your time!

ABENDA: Anytime, man, come on!

CHAPTER 2

Starfood Café—UCL Finals Game

ANNOUNCER: Douglas Costa, dribbling his way around Barca's defense. Pike looks defenseless. Costa to Cuadrado … a quick center from the left flaaaank to … Cristiano Ronaldoooo … goaaalazooo!

- Yes, yeeees.

- Yeaaaahh! Woah, this boy is the best.

BARTENDER: You're right, boy! I like his skills, definitely.

On this early afternoon, in the midst of a hot, sunny summer day, the shades of the young maple trees outside of the Starfood Café, along with the green-roofed tents planted on the deck, were offering a cooling effect that only an AC system could match in the inside. Besides, this outside feeling of freshness had the upside of having a touch of nature. The spacious deck was entirely covered with many square guest tables, each surrounded by beautifully decorated chairs, mostly aureate, which made the whole place appear like an ever-bright scene, day or night, with or without the people occupying it. In this era of persistent pandemic, the public health-and-safety rulings held it that all dining settings would have to operate entirely outside. This afternoon, Starfood was packed with noisy and merry soccer fans watching through the hours and cheering along their respective teams and stars on display. Starfood was really buzzing in a feisty ambiance such that it was hard to pull a private conversation, yet Nobola and Abenda found a way to entertain a topic obviously dear to them and relevant for the epoch while sharing a thought every now and then with Don, the bartender. They had managed to pick a table by the corner of the deck closest to the bushy rosy garden and opposite to the street. Here, the magnificent quiet of the plants, occasionally interrupted by a few bird cries, seemed to defiantly ward away the bulk of the noise from the restaurant's crowd.

"CR7 is so good, I've told my son the only way I would keep watching his soccer games is when he begins to show skills like CR7's," Don went on.

ABENDA: I see! And Starfood also is the best place to eat and to watch CR7's games.

NOBOLA: Oh yeah, Starfood's reputation for mixing good eats, good news, and entertainment is unparalleled

ABENDA: Sure, but it's hard to watch BNN here these days, which used to be the staple channel years ago …

BARTENDER: Just because all they have to say now is a bunch of crap. Everything they say is so biased.

ABENDA: You have not been showing much of the other popular cables either ...

NOBOLA: Don is right, many of these cables are the ultimate mirrors of one another, especially the ones with far left and progressive political opinion views ... so partisan and filled with fake news. Hah!

ABENDA: As far as I'm concerned, you, John, particularly have been so keen recently to making sure all leftists' butt are kicked.

NOBOLA: True, and trust me, I wish I had a better platform to say everything and all the truth about them, 'cause seriously, they are now getting on my nerves.

ABENDA: Okay! Relax, my brother, I don't mind getting you a nice platform soon.

CHAPTER 3

Forum for Grassroots and Emerging Patriots

NOBOLA: What? Wow! Finally, a place I've seen in recent memory that looks and feels like America. Wow, this is fantastic.

Nobola was relatively new in Magaville, and thanks to Abenda, he was discovering one of the somewhat secluded yet very lively places in the city.

People of all walks of life came here to speak or listen every day, any time. Food and drinks of all kinds and taste were provided infinitely for a stipend, or sometimes gratis for those who could not afford paying. Other accommodations that were available included toilets, a gym, and a multidisciplinary open playground. In the midst of it all was the US forum: Magaville, a big stage that had given its name to the place itself; it was where Americans who stood for the defense and enhancement of the ideas set up by their founding fathers came and left each day at a time of their convenience. Situated in the outskirts of the city's urban areas, the forum was part of a huge park that drew the wildest contrast possible with the busy and buzzy life of the city.

The forum hence seemed conceived to conform to the quiet that reigned in the park. Its stage stood down in the middle of a hemi-amphitheater, styled after the Greek-era structures. Planked on a big hillside, the whole place was recognizable by the big array of huge American flags raised so close to one another, circling the entire area and so tall they competed for attention with the dark, leafy secular trees of the park.

ABENDA: Great! I thought you would wanna see how this place fits in your plans to unleash on the demagogues of the leftist politics. Patriots convene here year-round, putting ideas together for a fight, recently renewed, to hold up American values against surging anarchist and socially destructive movements. Whenever you are ready, you will be able to get here and display what you have in stock against phony and misleading politicians.

NOBOLA: It sounds good. But first let's go home and prepare to vote on Tuesday's district elections.

CHAPTER 4

Vote Check

Piinng, puuung, piinng…

Nobola had left his office early that sunny Tuesday afternoon, a day deemed essential for the election year. Otherwise called special Tuesday, it was that day local jurisdictions held elections to renew or fill up vacancies for various government and educational leadership positions.

Nobola was hoping to beat the unusual traffic in his neighborhood's normally quiet and fluid Blankfield Street. However, today was different, and the road was packed. The polls closing time was fast approaching, and Nobola didn't want to miss the opportunity to make his voice heard in this important moment of his community's life. His nice white shirt now was soaked from a profuse transpiration he could hardly control when repeatedly wiping his face with the paper napkins he always kept in his truck's glove box. Cars in front of him were slow but moving, and luckily enough, at this point in time, the poll's location was a short distance away.

Nobola got there a few minutes before close. Abenda was waiting for him; he had cast his own vote a little earlier, and because of the difficulty finding a parking spot now, he agreed with Nobola that he would leave only to allow him to park and vote. It worked. The line to the polls was still there, but not as huge as Nobola had feared. He cast his vote, then he joined Abenda as they headed for a quick stop at the Starfood to relax and have a discussion about the day.

ABENDA: Who did you vote for?

NOBOLA: Man, I voted Republican all across the board!

ABENDA: Really! So why did you do that?

NOBOLA: The Dems are getting on my nerves! I have told you they are, wherever or whoever they are! All they want is grab the power, for themselves and their party.

ABENDA: Hey, John, you can't say that. Many, probably most of these people, may be cryingly eager to use and abuse political privileges to their advantage. But remember, to any rule, there are exceptions!

NOBOLA: Did you find one of these exceptions as you voted Dems again? So we are going back to the discussion we had last time, right, brother? The premise from Déjà vu that we black folks are born to vote one way without questioning, generation after generation, father to son to grandson. It's like a curse, isn't it?

ABENDA: Look, bro, no one has ever condemned us to be that way. Many circumstances, past or contemporary, have justified that we often stick together. Nonetheless, reality changes with times, and people don't have to lean their thoughts one single way and blindly because of their color. Since the end of the slave trade, black people are free from tyranny and exploitation, not only from the outside oppressors, but from those in their own communities as well. That is called freedom and includes free opinion!

NOBOLA: Should I now conclude that you hence voted Dem freely?

ABENDA: No, bro, but also I didn't have to anoint all candidates with their exclusive party blessing. I believe in good leadership that doesn't stop at the party line. Therefore I picked some good Dems and some good Reps for this election. Remember, we are here at a local level. Meaning, we and our kids are directly affected by who we choose to lead our community. We know who we vote for first hand, and we ought to decide meticulously.

NOBOLA: Well said, my brother. I still can't stand how some of our fellow countrymen were let down during a terrorist attack of a United States embassy in Africa, under the watch of the Democratic administration, how the left-leaning press had used its powers to protect the Democrat leaders and their partisan interests over the interests of the public and the country, and I have turned my back to the Dems forever!

ABENDA: Unfortunately, I am noticing the absurd politicization of every important issue, like the novel virus, and the polarization of all political opinions these days.

NOBOLA: I know people tend to ignore the importance of being decent with every debate, be it political or not. It takes very little for some to call Potus, our president, the new Hitler. When recently, the country was drowning in disgust after an awful murder of a citizen by the police, the president called for all to come together in "a time for healing" and to avoid division. He asked his advisor to remind everyone of these words from M. L. King, that during challenging times, we must stand together as one nation "or perish together as fools."

"He wouldn't have said such things," one colleague at work that day said to me. "Where did you hear that?" she asked me with some interest.

"From the Telefax News channel," 1 answered.

"Really? If this information is not from BNN, I don't believe it," she said.

"Well, do you just know how much fake news comes from BNN?" I asked her.

"After all, the president is a dumb man, he wouldn't say such nice things," she replied.

At that point, I was really upset and told her, "You cannot be serious and just insult the president of the greatest nation on earth each time you disagree! It's an insult to the very majority of the people who elected him!"

"You know what, he is not my president!" she said.

"He is my president, and the official and elected president of the United States!" I replied.

"That means you like him … because you are dumb like him," she said.

I held my breath, and my mouth opened up as she turned her back and walked away. I could hardly believe she had just told me those words. I stared at the empty space for a while longer, then I thought, *At least she is gone.* You see that kind of feeling?

ABENDA: I try to imagine, my friend, but enough politics for now. Let's enjoy Starfood's great coffee!

CHAPTER 5

Pleas on Broken American Experiences

At the Forum, Nobola and his friend had managed to secure a slot that would give Nobola the opportunity to voice his thoughts against the despicable new culture of shaming American values. In recent weeks, they had seen many symbols of the nation's history vandalized by so called "peaceful protesters," among other acts of destruction. Widespread waves of violent demonstrations went by, orchestrated by these rioters with the blessing of the Dems party leaders, who mostly preferred to ignore their destructive actions, supported by their left-leaning mass-media backers.

Nobola would be allowed to bring his plea for the defense of American conservative and traditional values on a schedule that he deemed convenient, without any type of pressure. It was the same order of intervention for everyone, depending on the availability of slots. Intervenients were patriotic activists or anyone else that had a say on the flow of sociopolitical economic events of the country.

The audience was all set; many people often attended personally on their spare time as the hemi-amphitheater almost always appeared to hold full capacity. The broadcast was available for those who opted to listen online, over the air, or to watch on TV instead.

Nobola chose to come in the first three days successively and wanted to proceed thereafter as the circumstances permitted.

A

Before Day 1

NOBOLA: I have a concern: as I already told you multiple times before, more and more people among us see their dreams go in flames.

ABENDA: I know! These days, black folks are constantly told what political expectations are for them: to say yes to everything, always go with the flow of the situation as painted by the news, mostly fake from the left activists. For you and me in particular, upon coming to America, the prospect of living in a dream country was a clear and nice choice. The America that we knew about and that, for a good first few years, proved its worth, was that mighty Land of the Free, founded on the most respected and fairest constitutional ground ever on earth: a society of so many dreams come true, most of which any human society has ever witnessed, and the envy of the whole world.

Like any human society, America has its own flaws, but they are self-contained. Its social values are constantly thriving to evolve for the best, as they are kept embedded within the keen and solid umbrella of a well-oiled political system of checks and balances. America came to be the best place to dwell in, with such great social harmony while housing such a diverse nation. Fortunately enough, the greatness of the people has rooted itself in everyday life, which is the fruit of the Founding Fathers' hard work, and of the sweat and tears of many following them, who did their best to preserve the founders' ideals. The effort has followed up with today's average American living his or her life in appreciation; the latest does so, yes, sometimes through hardships but knowing that tomorrow almost always, brings a better outlook.

In this America, everyone indulges their luck or takes their daily pill in good fairness. Oh yeah, John, sometimes I think about current events and really, I begin to understand your concerns.

NOBOLA: so I was just going to ask, is this America, the one you just described, heading out the door now?

ABENDA: I wouldn't say so. Nonetheless, we may still face an important hurdle until some of us understand the worth of sticking with this country through good and trying times. To become an American coming from a foreign country is not an easy feat. For many, having part of their family already implanted here can make the process smooth. Not always the case for others whose best reason to stay is the ever-promising horizon of hope. For these, to just be physically present on the country's soil constitutes not only a big first step but also the actual reality of their dream. Am I correct?

NOBOLA: Definitely! No matter how we come, a great majority among us starts their journey to the American dream as illegal immigrants. Fortunately, illegal immigrants are not that scary plague to be disposed of at first sight; the US legal frame provides rules that protect aliens of all kinds, whereas other legal outlets guarantee methods and processes to follow in order, over time, to reach recognition as a fully law-abiding American citizen.

ABENDA: Right! Many of us start up as illegals and find it gratifying to undergo the legitimation process, sometimes through extenuating challenges, but knowing that there is a way forward.

NOBOLA: Can you clarify?

ABENDA: Yes. I think it is humbling to go through legal hurdles because of the needed respect for the law and those in charge of law enforcement. It's even more reassuring to understand that the laws of the land, in fact, provide protection for those whose unlawful presence would have otherwise meant insecurity.

In other words, if you are an alien, you want to give some respect to the effort it took you to succeed at finding refuge under such a good and decent legal umbrella, and stand strong for protecting the umbrella so it would work even smoother in the future, not trash or destroy it, as would recommend some anarchist progressists nowadays.

Nobola thought it was a good idea to have a thorough conversation with friends and family on his concerns well before taking the issue to the general public. So this Sunday, after a morning of jogging in the park, Abenda and himself sat at his backyard's porch to take a look one more time into their plan to enter the forum.

The delightful sensations from the breeze that blew straight into their faces felt totally paradisiac. They had just drunk plenty of fresh water and now were sipping in the tasty ginger-and-lemon tea, a specialty Nobola had borrowed from Benson, a Jamaican friend of his. Nobola had now made a cult of taking it every morning and called it his gut-keeper.

All of the sudden, they heard a noisy conversation coming from the living room. Then, *kzzeaaann...* a door opened.

They were soon joined by Marty, Nobola's wife, who had just come back home from church.

MARTY: Honey! How was the workout today?

NOBOLA: Not bad. Isaac is here with me.

MARTY: Hey, Isaac, how are you doing?

ABENDA: Great! You are looking awesome, and your church dress is great! Please enjoy some gut-keeper with us!

MARTY: Thanks! But today I am not the only to gavage your brother's horrible concoction.

She smiled, looking coquettishly and glancing alternately at Nobola and Abenda, as Nobola stared afar in apparent disdain.

NOBOLA: Marty, I don't even have time for your BS today.

MARTY: Come on, honey, don't get mad! You know I love your effort to put something on the table, that's what matters to me.

She went on smiling, as Abenda smiled back graciously.

NOBOLA: So who did you bring home today, Marty?

MARTY: Mamatee, Mamyso, and their kids.

"Please come to the back everyone!" Marty called. Hellos followed, then all holding each other's hand, they stood around the tea table and went in unison: "In the name of the Father and the Son, and the Holy Ghost, Amen. Our Father who is in heaven …".

It was a family tradition that every Sunday after church, designated church members would visit each worshipper's home in support and solidarity for one another. Mamatee was one of the church choir's leaders; Mamyso and Marty were both co-assistant chairs in charge of social networking.

Soon the prayers were over, and all kids were dismissed to go to the play area in the yard. The adults remained seated at the table to think one more time on Nobola's new favorite topic.

ABENDA: Dear ladies, we were just having a conversation about ongoing social turmoil and political dissent in the country. Where do you stand on these issues?

MAMYSO: There are so many conflicts of opinions within our people. The least I can say is, we need some love, tolerance, and understanding in this country. Like the priest always says, "Love thy neighbors as thyselves."

MARTY: Mamyso! These words are not from the priest, Christ Jesus said them out of his own mouth.

MAMYSO: Well, how does that matter?

MAMATEE: It does because the impact of the words will always depend on who says them. Besides, our beloved priest is good, but I don't see him, as a human being, leading examples such as those of our Lord Jesus Christ.

NOBOLA: You are right, Mamatee, you know why? Because many of these preachers are just like politicians, especially from the left; they know how to talk the talk but hardly ever walk the walk.

MAMYSO: Nonetheless, the words are important, but the intention is what matters most. Some good, wise person from the past is advising us to listen to and do what they say, and not necessarily do like they do ...

ABENDA: Yes, I agree!

MAMYSO: Alleluia!

NOBOLA: Talking about walking the walk, don't you all appreciate the walk our great president took from his palace, with the Bible in his hands, to one of our churches being burned down by "peaceful protesters"? This president showed he can brush politics aside and stand for each one of us, including the faithful.

MAMYSO: You're right. This country is built on the intangible faith of its sons and daughters in our God Almighty, and attacks on places of worship are the most despicable thing I can ever imagine.

NOBOLA: And guess what Mamyso? In this country, you have a group of politicians who are going to defend such horrific actions no matter what.

MAMYSO: I've heard of them a lot from friends and in the news. So I've decided, next election, they are not getting my vote. Sometimes I even wonder if, in the name of political power, these people may have forgotten about God. They advocate murdering babies in their mothers' wombs, they don't like the laws of their country—the same laws that allow them to rise to the heights they are showing off from. Most of the time, they say many things that sound interesting but which they never accomplish.

NOBOLA: Brothers and sisters, I am telling you one more time. We now have a president who does not handle the business of politics like many politicians these days. He doesn't stop at talking, he does what he promises. He wants to defend this country from falling into the decline of deception by unethical politicians. We must all join Mamyso and defeat his opponents! Alleluia!

MAMATEE: Yes, ooooh?

MAMYSO: Yes.

MARTY: Yes!

MAMATEE: Let's pray …

They all stood around the table and held hands, listening to a few worshipping words, mostly praising and thankful to the Lord. All said "Amen," and the Sunday visit came to an end.

All the women hastily retreated back toward the living room as they appeared to rush and finish up some lady type of business.

Meanwhile, Nobola and Abenda remained at the porch, eager to resume their talk.

NOBOLA: You did evoke something about attacks on the legal system. What do you think is happening?

ABENDA: People are encouraged to disrespect the laws, and in many instances, those in charge of implementing them, up to the point, view immigration rules as needing to disappear, not enforced or reinforced. Movements even exist to support the concept of open borders into the US because there is some kind of political benefit they get from such an abomination. Do you just recall any other country with open borders in the world?

How do these kinds of movements help the debate on immigration? Not much. Instead, they make a traditional issue that has over the years found respectable venues of resolution, more complex. The immigrants do hence appear to increasingly have a suspicious presence for many. Immigrants, legal or not, have always been a necessary force for the progress and success of the nation. They live in an already too delicate situation to make it more uncomfortable thanks to senseless partisan policies.

Nobola: How do we end up with inadequate and controversial policies, where normally we should expect as a Democratic country to be guided by law and order?

Abenda: There are many practices, actually unlawful, most of the time erected and defended by certain local officials from the Democratic Party. They include sanctuary cities and other sorts of in limbo rules for immigrants. They probably don't foster a context in which one would want to live; they are often without a foreseeable solution for the illegality of one's status.

Nobola: As far as I know, and based on the Dems' line of thought, temporary rules are some of the most effective ways to help illegals out.

Abenda: Well, I believe instead the Dems, through these practices, help themselves and their partisan agendas first. No one wants to live in limbo and probably not so infinity. Besides, who's willing to live in limbo and depend for survival on the Dems' socialist-inspired welfare policies? Maybe not until you know who helped you to survive, then next time around, eventually, the guilt for you is to not vote for who "helped" you.

That's the other kind of dream you harvest if you come to America. The formation of the Democratic Party's base takes place this way. And my feeling is, some mental hijacking must have happened along the way.

Nobola: What?!

Abenda: What do you think, that people like Dems are so good they just wanna do you good?

Nobola: No, brother, I just think you are now beginning to sound like me.

B

Day 1 at the Forum: Partisan Rhetoric and Hijacking of Immigrants' Dreams

"Is the American dream fading? For many, especially young, mostly millennials, living in the US do not resound with the same vibe of the promising horizon we used to be attracted to. Because of various so-called progressist ideas erected by the Dems and implanted in the minds of the youth, they don't seem to have any problem questioning the social values they inherited from their parents. In short, many like to hate America, its culture, and its leaders, particularly any president who stands for American traditions of pride and might.

"This tendency is not new to Potus's presidency. It is now more than ever exacerbated, but was long in the making. By the logic of the Democrat ideology, all schemes are good whenever they help to display a Republican president with the darkest aura. They promote all kinds of denigrating of the president, regardless if this hurts the country's image or if it means blatant disrespect for an elected official's authority, leading to the spread of rebellious tendency in the minds of many unprepared people and the social disharmony that may ensue. Another Republican president before Potus used to be tagged with sinning by not speaking English like fourteenth-century London dwellers. In "heavily democrat" (by D. J. Trump) constituencies such as those in MD or DC, he could be blamed for anything despite his accomplishments, including the post-9-11 period, when he took important steps to keep the country's spirits up. He was known to take shots from every big or little bunch of the society, and people would make fun of him as the least intelligent person of the whole earth.

"Heavily democrat cities and states are well renowned for harboring a good deal of the newest immigrant populations. The Dems' propaganda is readily available to these populations, feeding them up with the distorted idea that it is cool to vow disrespect for the person of the president in America. Because of limited experience of the society, the new immigrants often embrace that tendency as a sign of freedom. The lack of, or limits to the opportunity for, unbiased, discerned, and plural information keeps them in this kind of mindset for a long time. If you are a new immigrant living in a blue state, your chances of getting mentally surrounded, buried, and crushed in this environment are heightened. It is the mighty blue political and social cloud that is truly very hard to escape.

"The trend is obvious again with today's Potus presidency. Its intended or sometimes unintended consequences are certainly a great boon for the progressivists and anarchist politicians, but not necessarily for America. These consequences include the following:

- Extension and reinforcement of the Dems base.
- Rewriting the immigrant's political purpose of embracing the American culture by inciting people to oppose and fight it instead.
- Creating an American enemy from within and without, through importation of hypocritical and bigotry-filled immigrant waves that end up surviving, in some cases, multiple generations of their descendants.

"It all culminates up in today's culture of hatred for a great president and a world's very respected leader, one of the most pragmatic and people-relating politicians of our century. The end result is, one, to blind the immigrant's mind from the perceived opportunity that was the primary justification for coming to America: greatest economy, greatest education, and greatest mix up of people.

"Two, to steal the immigrant's long quest for joy and free enterprise to focus him or her on a new cycle of mind struggles that often reminds them of the struggles that they fled leaving their motherlands.

"When America is portrayed as a place of economic and social discomfort by the Dems and their allies in the mainstream media, despite intangible proof of the contrary, it all sounds like a confusing message to the ear of many who finally found peace after escaping social misery from other countries. Situations that fuel social unrest are a reason to now wonder if the American dream is turning into a new nightmare.

"The bottom line is, this is the kind of environment that Dem politicians thrive on. Their success depends so much on a world of misery. They get elected thanks to people who always complain about something and are never thankful for anything— the same who ignore God and his good deeds. They see freedom as a green light for doing or becoming anything, even through destruction of society or themselves. They are anarchists; they hate life, religion, traditions, order, and authorities. They like abortion and sex disorientation. They bypass values such as truth and fairness in order to influence vulnerable people.

"Are you an immigrant, or a descendant thereof, who is always told that nothing good ever comes from Potus or any Republican president, that nothing is right for you other than what you're being told by Dems, and that in a free country, you are actually not entitled to free opinion because you are considered an ignorant if what you know is not input from the leftist media? This type of propaganda has the ability to stick then spread for a long time, creating waves of frustrated, misinformed, deluded, and American-hating people.

"For many immigrants, a key element in the way they are introduced to the American political culture is, the process depends on many factors including their means of entry in the country (legal or illegal), the status the immigrant is granted based on the visa type, etc. Every immigrant's experience may differ from one another. The reality is, there is an ideological current guiding the process, if not many such currents.

"Many actors drive those currents: the government through the vetting procedures and other diplomatic maneuvers or enticements, the educational circles promoting certain social or economic perspectives, and most importantly, family or close relationships. The latest category is the channel in which partisanship is more likely to align with the choice of going to America.

"Are Dems more active than Reps when it comes to exploiting those currents or even going their own straight ways in order to win the immigrant's allegiance? It depends on who you ask. Nonetheless, for many, the brainwashing starts even as the target is not certain of ever traveling to the US. Many anecdotal accounts, of life abroad, to countrymen left behind, have culminated in the abuse of hard-to-control waves of fake news, the main instigators of which are known to have some level of interest in spreading. Such stories state that life in America is so smooth you don't even need to work. Others say that only Dems run social programs; some others that each time there's a Dem as president, all illegals turn citizens. They tell that, on the other hand, all migration stops with a Republican president, who then goes on to deport any illegal immigrant. These tales can actually be extended.

"The question is, do migrants always realize what is happening to them? Probably not, and often for a long shot. What happens when they do? Given that they hardly find a way of getting a real grab on actual aspects of the American culture because things are confusing? Sometimes something, sometimes nothing. Many times, it's easier to turn around and find refuge in the old ways of the culture of origin. A lot of people prefer not to take hard shots at life situations. For those, the flash of hope that led them to travel consists of ideas like finding free money falling off street trees once in the US. Then the sweet prospect is all gone with the same flash once they face the reality that prosperity comes with some effort. Disappointed and blinded by thoughts secreted by the previously mentioned tales, they tend to believe that only Dems can bail them out into their perceived dreams, thanks to the usual array of freebie programs.

"Dems may be well willing; they can present sound policies—don't get me wrong! But available and vulnerable minds are a quick find in a vast and rich electoral mine such as clusters of ambitious but politically unsecure new immigrants. Good or bad, right or wrong tactics? Anyone's guess. Can Reps keep up with the Dems on this? What can the government do?"

Following his presentation at the forum, Nobola was both exalted and exhausted by his performance. Despite many requests in the audience to take a few questions, he begged everyone to be lenient and opted to refer those with questions and comments to the follow-up discussion on social media. For many these days, this was becoming more and more a good alternative way of clarifying ideas. Leaving the stage under a good round of applause, he went home transported by his friend, Abenda.

He opened the little wooden gate to his house and waved goodbye to Abenda. Soon his wife and their kids came running as they hugged and cheered him.

MARTY: Honey, you did very good! We watched the whole thing on the live video broadcast.

NOBOLA: Thanks! I will go back tomorrow.

MARTY: I know my darling. Your dinner is ready. You take a quick shower. And once you eat, you have plenty of time to rest before tomorrow.

NOBOLA: You are right …

C

Day 2: Flip the Colors

"We people of black descent have been for so long defined or influenced by the black-and-white aspects of the society, examples of which are colonists versus indigenous, white masters versus black slaves, desolate mass of crippled poor versus 1 percent rich, etc. All kinds of attributes or qualifiers bearing thereof tend to encase us, almost always, on the losers' side—that of misery. In England, this describes what is considered the woke movement, an integral part of which is "the critical race theory" (speech by Kemi Badenoch, www.teaparty247.org,Oct 24, 2020). The theory has long been outlawed as criminal by the British.

"Is it ever soon enough to reconsider after recognizing our extreme dependence on the mental downfalls created by such clichés? Many among us tend to identify as the lot of the victims always needing the massive social mercy that comes with the nice and easy life procured by government assistance. We are often seeking consolation and retribution.

"When we are stuck as a collective into that kind of mindset, then we become the easy-to-reach and covert trouve of any political or activist group.

Politicians don't always have our best interests in mind; it's usually theirs first. They manipulate us; they remind us, depending on the circumstances, of where we belong (in the hell of poor) and of how they are best equipped to save us from sorrow.

"Terrorists, anarchists, and other extremists now infiltrate black-initiated movements, exploiting and infecting otherwise noble causes in order to create havoc around town. On the softer side, Dems in the US are the best harvesters of black and other minority voters. How? They use these people's problems to blind them with the illusion that only Dems can find solutions. They don't really fix problems. They like when the people are crushed by problems, which helps them to exist politically. They are relics of Communism and slavery-based politics.

"Our vote can hence be taken for granted at any time. So how do we think for ourselves now and out into the future if the way our opinions of ourselves and those pinned upon us by others keep us stuck in our miseries, past and present? If we want to have and control more political, economic, and social power pushing us through the future of universal mankind's equality, we must have and stand for opinions that go beyond black and white, Reps and Dems, powerful and powerless. 'How do you have power if you are not entitled to your own opinion?' was the question Kanye West asked recently. Also, Kim Klacik not long ago added that for blacks 'to pursue the goal of enduring freedom,' they need to belong 'on both sides of the isle.'

"We are people of color, hence we should excel at appreciating the colorful diversity of our American society, where we find glamorous coexistence; we don't benefit much from constantly dwelling in the black-and-white biased approach to life, which keeps us psychologically crippled and stuck in our past nightmares, especially when we keep ourselves on the outside, refusing to engage and belong.

"America, its society and its constitution, gives us a wonderful platform to a freedom-loving world. Many of us—black, white, Hispanic, Muslims, Indian, Arabic, Asian—came all eyes open to appreciate the vast ocean of possibilities and opportunities in this land, hoping to thrive in its beautiful and welcoming society. We have found unending successes within all layers of its vibrant people, through economic enterprise, sports, music, and education. We have oftentimes taken full advantage of the American dream. We ought to give this America a chance to always serve us its beauty so we can unequivocally rejoice in it."

"So what made you start up the question of colors today?" Abenda asked as Nobola and he rode their way out of the forum, just like the day before. The second-day presentation turned out to be relatively shorter than the first day, and they agreed to use the extra time to hang out and talk the rest of the day.

NOBOLA: Well, there's a promise of getting America back to its glory and greatness, presented by the government in charge at the moment. All Americans deserve to experience and live the reality of that promise, and though the Dems' base would deliberately disagree, it is not a partisan endeavor. The goal is to get each and every one on board with the train to the prospects, which were pursued by our constitution and our founding fathers.

ABENDA: But the constitution is a collection of words on paper, and the founding fathers are no longer alive. How do you reconcile that fact with times and today's reality?

NOBOLA: That's the exact purpose of maintaining law and order, without the manipulatory tendency that is common ground among left-leaning politicians and scholars.

ABENDA: Would you think of the constitution as the "covenant" that all freedom-loving people like to look up to?

NOBOLA: Thank you, brother! Think about it.

By this time, they had pulled over at a local 7-Eleven and sat at a bench inside. Nobola was sipping in his second cup of Coke, whereas Abenda chose to go with Pepsi, as usual. They liked to talk about politics; they were often caught discussing all sorts of issues by their friends and family to the point of being known as the two pundits.

Nobola went on, "America is the destination of many around the world. Each one of us comes or grows up here being aware of the liberties and opportunities this country has, which are guaranteed by laws that the Founding Fathers laid down. Freedom and opportunity belong in this greatest nation on earth that was built, thanks to the hard work of our ancestors. Your point of saying that those people are no longer here is interesting. However, every generation of Americans has the duty to keep their views and values alive, and pass them along to their descendants.

"We must continue the work of our ancestors, and protect and safeguard the text and spirit of the laws they had laid down.

ABENDA: John, this is easier said than done. Times change and, with them, the people, generation after generation.

NOBOLA: I agree, but the spirit of the Constitution must not change. Keeping up with our fathers' vision is not a mere destination, it's a work in progress that requires all Americans to respect each other and our laws and authorities. Everyone cannot be expected to do the same thing or produce the same results, but we must always remember that we ride the same boat, going the same direction, and hence need to go together, covering one another's backs.

ABENDA: How do different people with various, sometimes opposite, realities and ways of life get one another's backs?

NOBOLA: It takes respect for one another, which comes with tolerance and understanding that no matter how different we may seem, we depend on one another. The weak and the strong, the rich and the poor, the savvy and the mentally challenged, the coach and the owner, the player and the fan—we are all in the same boat, this beautiful place. We save it against the waves, and we live, or we let it sink from lack of civility and we perish together.

ABENDA: I agree, man! Our differences and partisanship must bear their limits and serve their purposes, but living together while keeping America great should have no excuse. Now I have a question for you. You are hinting that Republicans rhetoric aims to make America great again (MAGA); Democrats, too, are

Americans. Are they not trying to make things better on their own way?

NOBOLA: I am not sure how good their intentions are. The fact is that the Dems' ideology is one that would deprive most of us from our cherished economic and social freedom. Dems want us to be ruled by the old fallen Communist regimes' policies. They want us to look like China and North Korea—or at least close, where the government grabs all the powers and controls all the riches, while the majority of the population, no matter how crippled, must abide by the rules without much to say or do. The outlook on such a situation is a possibility that average Americans become a bunch of needy people, sitting in a social hole, the relief from which can only be achieved by the saving hand of socialist-derived government-assistance programs.

Meanwhile Republicans, in their policies, dare to challenge Americans of all origins to rise to the occasion of freely, courageously, and equally grasping the vast realm of opportunities offered by the Land of the Free and the Home of the Brave, without all the governmental strings holding anyone back.

ABENDA: From my understanding, the latter path very likely allows everyone to live their lives as they choose, to rip the fruits of their efforts proportionally to their merits, and not have to hold tight while they wait, uneasy, for every Christmas gift government would decide to make available or impose.

NOBOLA: Yep, you got it! At the end of the day, the settling answer resides in who makes the ultimate choice of defending the best interests of this nation over any kind of partisan divisive approach. Love of country tops love of party, and the party that loves America more than their ideology gets the trust of the people.

D

Day 3: In Mobs We Lost

"Today's life is filled with disasters perpetrated by anarchist mobsters who use every pretext to promote chaos. The situation is unsettling for everyone, at the exception of the politicians on the left and their allies from the mainstream media. They sow misinformation about current events in order to ensure the president is blamed for everything. They encourage and bank on people's ignorance, fueling illusion, delusion, and indoctrination in a purely partisan anarchist opposition.

"Ironically, they turn a blank eye on when not applauding acts of American economic and cultural destruction.

"As a migrant who has long found refuge in a cool American home after leaving a country that was embattled in civil unrest and economic misery, it is hard to see images of such a reality that has become common place on TV. To people like me, all they remind us of is that the risks of exposing our own children to this same scenario we had wished to spare now grow every day, exponentially.

"I believe and hope, with the coming presidential election, that America will soon choose between two options, the one that strongly stands for the defense of the values that the US rose from with pride: life, liberty, and the pursuit of happiness versus the one that shameless calls for doom and destruction around us every time.

"Fortunately, every day we find strong voices to foster the true America of our dreams, in Potus, M. Levin, Hannity, Rush, and many others. Various black figures from past and present demonstrate that we are not just a lucky found bunch that is always a lock for Democrats' voting percentages. These figures find their way into America's political and other aspects of public life, away from the Dem Party ties. They're those who have shown that blacks can freely think for themselves even when some consider them as sold out to sports and brainless money. They are the everyday Kanye West, Kim Klacik, and others. MLK's vision for a better America where we live together as brothers have no price. He accurately warned us to live together in peace or "perish together as fools." Jesus Christ knew better when he taught us to love each one of our neighbors as ourselves.

"Brown lives matter. Black lives matter. White lives matter. Latino lives matter. Blue lives matter. As for each one of us, longing for justice in all aspects of life, we must often set our sights on the long term, for only truth can set us free, not the emotional and partisan outbursts of the moment. It is the truth that is based on and translates the intention of the Founding Fathers of this great nation. We must fight any principle or attempt to destroy that truth, because the prospects that it carries into our lives are sacred, and that's what makes America special.

"As for America-loving migrants like myself, it is about time we call out and fight off all tactics brought to us by the mobsters, the result of which is no less than hijacking our hopes for a dream life in America. These tactics come with all sorts of horrors. They include intimidation, character assassination, fear mongering, name calling. They are the hallmark of many Democrats' political messages that help them to, successfully or not, hang on the power grip while emboldening America's enemies inside and abroad: thousands who hate our peace, brotherhood, diversity, freedom, probably, and the American way of life.

"Chaos is rampant on our streets! Countless churches and other places of worship are burnt to the ground! An American flag is torched as certain bystanders applaud and laugh! Private and public properties are destroyed, then looted! Monuments are vandalized—this can't be the US, but, yes, it is. The hailed model of civility and democracy, now being put to shame. Do the mobsters only reckon how much America is admired and envied abroad? Scenes of unrest are typical of our impoverished countries of origin. We ran away from them, and having to face them once again in America, that's not what we signed up for!"

It was midday, and today was looking to be another full, busy day for Nobola at the forum. But unlike the first two days, he agreed to take the optional lunch break. He walked off the stage to meet Abenda; there were many people applauding and multiple hands waved him thumbs-up, along with cheers of "Nice, great, good job!" Abenda soon joined him, and they were on their way out to the food court.

NOBOLA: I am gonna get myself a fish sandwich from McDonald's.

ABENDA: Ok, I like to eat fresh, so I am going to Subway instead.

NOBOLA: No problem, bro, so be it, and let's meet at this corner table once you get your order.

ABENDA: All right.

They ate fast enough. At twelve thirty-five, they were back inside the forum, just in time for Nobola to resume his presentation.

"Shots are constantly taken against America. The shooters launch unfriendly attacks on the American culture. They don't like to see us proud. They hate American products, especially cars. They are always laughing when the US men's soccer team fails. They praise American enemies and competitors. They are against ingredients for individual success that include merit, hard work, and critical thinking, and like Communists, they pretend that we must coexist in a world where all lead the same lives, no matter our differences. Has such a world ever succeeded, be it in the Vatican or even in our own families? We are entitled to equal rights, but we cannot have an equal livelihood even if we wanted to! So why continue to pretend? That is hypothetical hypocrisy, and that's where the leftist politicians want to drag people into by all means possible.

"We ought to establish a responsible and affirmed basis for patriotic education of the people in order to protect American culture against its detractors. Dems get it too easy spreading unethical and divisive partisanship. They unfairly abuse our constitutional rights to free speech, assembly, and opinion to exacerbate and exploit social crises, focusing on making political gains instead of seeking solutions that serve the common good, unity, and solidarity among all citizens. Their actions prove how their attachment to their party supersedes their love, if any, for the country.

"How does this translate in the daily experience? More and more people buy into an abominable ideology of uncanny distortion of the American culture. Slowly but steadily, these people, often from foreign nations by origin, step unprepared into an arena of hatred. They are subsequently drawn back, as per some magically driven unconscious retro behavior, within the realm of promoting the very antiquated and despicable social values from the countries they ran away from. At the time, they normally had hoped to be fully absorbed into the American way of life, the one they had so dearly longed for. Once in the US, they are dragged in a totally different direction. Knowingly sometimes and sometimes not, their hopes are being hijacked.

"What follows is now old news: they join the ranks of mobsters, directly or indirectly, because the easy way is to blame it all on America. This becomes even easier given the support they have from the liberal opposition and the media behind them. Mobsters, liberal politicians, and the left-leaning press now form a tandem with only one goal in their sight: sow havoc until they totally gain power, and nothing else.

"A crisis arises in the black community, and their only approach is to make it look like, as always, black and white. As an example, we know the issue of police brutality could be dealt with as such, without any extrapolation, although many have assumed that there's a systematic problem of police just killing blacks. Bias in law enforcement targeting minorities probably exists, and bad cops, whenever they commit crimes in carrying their duty, must be held accountable. That said, it's worth recognizing that most cops do a good job of keeping America safe.

"Injustices affect people no matter their condition or their color. Many will certainly agree to making sure we all as one nation find and improve ways to address those issues without dividing us. Helping mobsters to ignite fire whenever an issue arises does not make our communities better. Terrible acts of destruction have been committed by anarchists and so-called "peaceful protesters." Why can't we trust our law enforcement and judicial institutions to bring back justice where there isn't? There have been mobs invading cities as they deemed empowered to grab this judicial duty. They have taken away lives and property. Yes, it's been true mobs, everywhere, and in mobs, we lost!

"Which person willing to live in a diverse but inclusive nation wouldn't want to point at the US as a destination of choice? This is the land where the notion of tolerance has met its challenges and yet is holding well. We are the country of free speech and cultural diversity. All is not perfect, but every day, we work hard to make America better and better.

"We ought to open our eyes and not destroy the peace and prosperity we luckily have harnessed. Or for some, maybe you want, for a few seasons, to flip the rules and migrate for real, not for a short vacation, in any other country. You will no doubt learn to know what you've got in America before it's gone.

"Now, it's time to wrap up on the deception of not only derailing unaware citizens into joining the left but also trying to revive the Communist ideology and serve it to America. From an immigrant perspective, we often learn, before coming to America, a great deal about the differences between capitalism and Communism. Moving to live in the US is a clear indicator for the preference this holds over going to Russia or China instead. As appealing as the Communist ideas, along with all related political, social, and economic doctrines may appear (Marxism, Engelism, Socialism, Socio-Democratism, etc.), they are all best known for their failures to translate into any successfully positive humanity experience. For illustration, the Berlin wall went down, USSR died, and China is trying hard to become relevant. Even in the golden years of Communism, scholars agreed that perpetual adjustments to the system were vital, given that parent ideologies, which are Marxism and Engelism, proved to be overly utopian. As a result, you end up with all sorts of failing derivatives to Communism. Capitalism must adapt to the times, don't get me wrong. But it remained capitalism and stood the test of time.

"Great achievements sometimes come with some opposition to the status quo, but opposition isn't welcome as only aiming to destroy what so meticulously has been built. Opposition ought to prove its value to deserve meddling with the sometimes controversial, but edifying and irreplaceable past."

CHAPTER 6

Where Do We Stand?

"The process of manipulation of well-intending people for the purpose of recruiting them into the leftist ideology found some level of success. Hate of the American people's reality in all occasions has led to dispersion of our wealth and talents while trying to fix other nations at our own expense. China since has gone superpower overnight thanks to the American industries being granted to them during the times many doubted the American citizens. Then, a weak and permissive stand of our foreign policy makers emboldened the likes of Russia and Iran, not their people, their freedom-chocking regimes. The former unlawfully grabbed vast territories in Eastern Europe with no one standing on their way. The latter moved closer and closer to nuclear-weaponry bragging rights.

"Furthermore, children of this country are subdued to an educational curriculum, critically strange to their parents, which mounts to convincing today's youth that they are citizens of a wrong nation; therefore, they must grow ashamed of their parents' cultures. No human society is perfect, yet young people are being taught that erasing and hiding from the controversial moments of their history is the way forward; instead, should they not be told to learn from such dark moments in order "to rise to the occasion "(MLK) and make the future better?

"Instead of using the social challenges of the past to unearth hatred and promote division among Americans to connect conflicting ideas and make a more beautiful environment of peace, tolerance, and healing for all?

"Instead of relying on the outbursts of destructive utopian movements to trust the spirit of God to keep us together as loving brothers and sisters?"

This day was when Nobola had chosen to undergo the optional questioning from the audience. He was facing people of all walks of life in the forum. Although he managed, after each presentation, to go over related social media followings and post-relevant comments or answers to questions, he thought today would be the best chance to address some of his topic's gray areas face-to-face.

Q: You mentioned a few times that the Dems hijacked immigrants away from the lives they had hoped for. How does this opinion specifically fit a black person like yourself into attempting or eventually convincing him or her to go blue?

NOBOLA: It's a process that comes with the induction of a question, or many questions at a time, in the mind of the person: am I black enough not to limit myself to watching TV without making TV? Am I African enough to not be an exclusive soccer fan who has no business to understanding and watching basketball or baseball or football? Am I not lazy enough not to be, by definition, made to look without ever questioning and maybe just shut up and dribble? Ignorant enough to not understand that my position in this country's politics is to vote Democrat or else I "ain't black"? Useless enough to not remain relegated as a locked voting percentage, a being whose position in society is assumed by prejudice and who is understood solely through the prism of his color no matter what he says or does? Am I sage enough to not oppose those who think that discrimination is here but has had its uglier past, and that all social frictions and intercultural fractions that survive are a predictable trait of a diverse nation, to not argue that American laws on justice and rules on equality are nothing but mere delusion, to not refute that I potentially have the same power to rise in life as anyone else despite my color or minority?

Am I colorful enough not to even refuse embracing contemporary social emancipation that recognizes today as new and yesterday as then, to believe that I don't have to live my parents' life, one so frustrating that the only survival mechanism I learned growing was to play defense? Am I even black enough to not just watch and ignore, because where I live and interact, only conformation is accepted?

So my friend, coming to a new land and living a new life, for me and many like me, has its share of unknowns. These create a terrain of vulnerability, and the people involved become a great political mine field where opportunistic deception as that from the left preys constantly on undecided minds.

Q: Today's America being a place where, knowingly or unconsciously, many of us are bounded by allegiance to our tribal communities, what does this allegiance do? Create microcosm of our cultures of origin and hence undermine harmony and integration?

NOBOLA: I bet giving our subcultural identities priority over the American flag comes easily just as promoting such tendency undermines national integration. But sometimes we must reckon the reality of multiculturalism and, for the sake of our communion through diversity, "rise to the occasion" (MLK) of that type of challenge to keep America a place where all are welcome and feel it.

Q: Do you oppose of blacks taking their fight against injustices out to the street?

NOBOLA: I don't. Instead, I disagree with those who use the fight to break the law and people's property. That's not the right way to carry the message. We must protest lawfully and peacefully or endure being marginalized by others as well as our own people, especially those victims of our criminal actions. It's not a sustainable strategy to be always on the outside, angry, polarized, and confrontational. We need our children to know that they are growing up where they belong, a free and loving place.

Q: Don't you think black children should learn to recognize abuse and fight back?

NOBOLA: Yes, we must teach them that we are a tough tropical species and will always remain set, ready to strike those who disrespect our lives. Still we must face our frustrations without losing reason, settle issues in context, according to the law and without setting our society ablaze.

Q: Can you give clarification on how leftists and their mobs relate to the existential questions you asked earlier?

NOBOLA: Every single person has those kinds of questions at some point of their life, I think. But given a context like that we face these days, leftists seize those moments to magnify doubt in the minds of people while stirring confusion, conflict, and division. On the other hand, another tool that the shameless politicians use is to present minority people's successes as panacea for their peers or admirers dreaming of a better life. With that in mind, many carry out their life as if the only way for them to count is to first be superstars of some sort, be it in sports, politics, arts, or other things.

That's in the mindset of a good number of minority recruits on the left. The leftists use people's miseries to ignite division, and successes to sow delusion. It is a masterful technique for sticking cast labels into society and, to some extent, for segregating, because it all comes down to saying either you are this or you are nothing: success or failure, star or useless, black or white, police or victim—nothing in between. And who is the mastermind of such a societal outlook, other than the Marxist-Leninist doctrine of social classes and their flag bearers in today's politics, the Dems?

Q: What do you think is the most worrisome thing about that outlook?

NOBOLA: So many among us have given in to that abstract and absurd shaping of the society. People have locked themselves into it to the point of not letting any window open to opinion differences, thereby denying all chances of dialogue and tolerance building. You could be bullied, shamed, colluded on, even insulted if not cursed with name calling or labeling, and it would be allowed as normal.

Q: Who's to blame?

NOBOLA: Bizarre and despicable behaviors have their origin in extremist ideology, which can flourish in the left as well as right wing of politics. Nonetheless, they now are overwhelmingly amplified by mainstream media because of the latter's devotion to the cause of anarchists. The hope through this whole propaganda is to ensure Potus is removed from power because of his strong stand against demagogues.

Q: Do you see any relationship of this propaganda with life outside of the US?

NOBOLA: For sure! This tendency doesn't stop only here. It spans through the rest of the world, where most have no choice but to bend below the liberal informational monopoly.

And the rest of the world manufactures a great deal of the new human apparatus that feeds the Dems' electoral core. Those in this category come to the US, not for the love of the country, but to use what we offer, promoting the betterment of causes abroad, yet definitely against the interests of the Americans. How much longer should patriots put up with that?

Q: Do you believe that extreme leftist policies are more responsible for social injustices than the right?

NOBOLA: Yes! Policies that despise ethics, law and order, and the fear of God have their roots in the exploitation of vulnerable people. They have been inspired by anarchists and, to some degree, Marxists in the past. Their intentions are clear as crystal yet have hardly ever been of any good use. Anarchists and imperialists used slavery to subdue foreigners for their own benefit, a practice that prevailed until the abolitionist movement came to be. In the process, the American Constitution declared that "all humans are created equal. Subsequently, the likes of A. Lincoln, a Republican, took a step further to defend freedom.

Marxists used the deception of casting masses of people with a fake approach to equality. Over the years, they produced millions of equally exploited and abused laborers, while their oligarchy of rulers racked up the benefits of the people's hard work. This until Ronald Reagan came along and helped put an end to Communism.

Colonists later after slavery, while ignoring teachings from the peace-oriented religious groups that came with them, made a duty to pillage others, mauling them with deplorable and divisive policies of destruction and deception. These policies are the same, by which Dems often rule. They indicate that society must absolutely have something wrong within, an idea that has circled the world, making many in underdeveloped countries believe that what they have at home is always of the least value. So these people are never satisfied with anything. And with secular conflicts and societal confusion, they live decades after decades in fear and insecurity. That's where many among us come from, thirsty for peace in the Land of the Free. May some of our foreign policies in the past have contributed to this outcomes? Could be, until Potus came to power.

He is different; he wants foreign nations and their peoples to believe in and enjoy their own lives, wealth, and cultures. He doesn't believe in an America that constantly polices others. He knows we are better off and therefore can help others out, but not at the expense of the American people and society, as is seen through irresponsible immigration movements by which some come not to enjoy and contribute good to America but to destroy it, like they do their own places of origin.

Q: Can we have a quick example of such policies applied by Potus?

NOBOLA: Potus! He doesn't mind if a country of Africa is ruled by a president, a king, or a chief; whatever works for those countries and their people, let it be! Some of these people understand, and you have the Bamotoland government who never shies away from bragging about the country's unique natural riches and gifts. Recently, I met with Massena, the head of the Bamoto congregation in the US, and he had this to say, "Our people come here to live the American dream, not to give trouble to America. Likewise we don't want to bring our own trouble and ask America to fix it. Because back home, they already know that 'xa se passe ici, chez nous sur place' (Petit Pays). The Bamoto are a proud people, despite some exceptions. Potus knows so much about such countries; and he treats them as sovereign nations, not American babies or property.

CHAPTER 7

What's in a Name?

Oof! Saturday was finally here. It had been a much busier week than usual. Because of the time spent on his forum's interventions, Nobola did not show up at his business planner office even a single time. Instead, he managed to complete his assignments remotely. He discussed various things with colleagues over the phone, including comments about his forum time. Today, temperatures were feeling mild and nice; the skies looked a little cloudy and overcast. As Nobola hung over the black pole of his front porch, he received a call from Asso, a colleague, reminding him of the dinner he was offering to mark his new baby's birth.

NOBOLA: Nice! I will be there in an hour. I will get ready, and I will be bringing my friend Abenda with me.

ASSO: All right, see you then!

At 1600, Nobola and Abenda arrived together at the Starfood. There, Asso and a few other friends were already sitting, enjoying the great food and drinks that Starfood was renowned for.

"So what name are you giving your new baby?" Ekiey, one of the guests, came to ask.

Asso: I am not sure yet.

Nobola: You know what folks, I had chosen and given my daughter her name, but I didn't realize it was an issue for some until I told them.

Ekiey: As far as you are concerned, almost everything comes down to politics, including newborn names policy.

Haahaahah! You could see the sitting guests throwing their feet out as all went hilarious.

Asso: You are right, Ekiey. He and Abenda serve us politics every day just like the ice cream trucker serves ice cream with Christmas songs!

Ekiey: Yeah, men, trust me. For these two, every day is political Christmas, hehehehe!

Abenda: No, but seriously, John, I have been long trying to ask you what really happened with you naming Ivy.

Ivy was the youngest of Nobola's three daughters. She was born on the day that Potus was being sworn in to his presidential mandate, and for Nobola and his wife, it was just as simple to name her after the new first daughter, as it was intuitive. Besides, Potus's daughter had the reputation of being a great family-loving woman; she was very attached to issues facing modern families and turned to become the best defender for social and family rights among her father's staff. After taking a quiet, deep breath, Nobola started: "I thought I could freely name my children any name I wanted, as long as my family and I deemed it fit for our approach to life. When Ivy came to the world, my wife and I decided to give her the name.

EKIEY: But you knew so many people disliked the president!

NOBOLA: Of course we did, but we didn't have to blindly agree with those people. Above all, the name is pretty, so why is it so much of a deal?

ASSO: Do you remember the popular saying "There's something in a name"?

NOBOLA: Yeah, I do. It didn't take me long to realize what was coming, luckily, long before Ivy herself would have gotten to realize anything, and she still hasn't.

ABENDA: What did you realize?

NOBOLA: At a neighborhood event, an acquaintance of mine, a nice middle-aged woman I used to talk to each time we met at the local tropical grocery store, approached me and whispered, "Ivy? You will regret that!" stunning to me it was. But I didn't want to worry about it.

EKIEY: Why not?

NOBOLA: Because I knew she was not threatening me, but instead wanted to translate her concerns with me naming my newborn after this president's daughter. So she went on to say, "That's a dangerous first name ... poor little one."

Calmly I responded, "I am okay with the name, but thank you."

Besides, I believe she wished so much I had chosen according to her advice. She was soon gone away, and I said to myself, with some disgust, as I watched her disappear in the middle of the crowded community hall: "Doesn't she wish I could have consulted with her, or others like her, about getting the "right" name for my child?

ABENDA: Your wife, Marty, and you didn't seem to agree on your opinions, especially relating to the condition of minorities in general. How could you agree to stuff about Potus?

NOBOLA: You are right. However, at the time, we were beginning to feel the crush of an entourage whose only goal was to gavage us up with talks about the hate for Potus on one hand and the merits of Democrat politics on the other. It was a constant blue cloud stuffing our minds and suffocating our spirits. We needed a way out.

Given the circumstances, we didn't have any extensive discussion on why Potus would have to be an inspiration for our family. In general, Marty, like myself, isn't a fan of dragging around great debates to tackle big issues. We like to rely on our guts, not on sophisticated and elaborate ideology, to choose what is right for us.

ABENDA: Wow, you are coming forward with a lot of new information about your sacred life with Marty!

NOBOLA: Oh yeah, it's beyond what you thought. We went straight with our intuition when we fell in love, despite our respective families' almost concerted reticence. We go by the same token when it comes to running our family life together. This includes the choice of saving each one of our kids once conceived, despite the appeal of planned-parenthood clinics and other unborn baby–murdering associations. We didn't need any special explanation to embrace a well-deserving first president of color; we were going to welcome Potus, despite unwarranted critics, as the next president of the highest office on earth that deserved all due respect for winning the electorate of the best democratic formula. Needless to say, Potus displayed overwhelming charisma and immense ability to relate to the greatest social issues of the moment. He knew how to connect with the average Americans and had long proved his understanding of the reality that faced most without distinction of race and without embellishment of his political tone. He had kept all his electoral promises to the American people. He wasn't recognized as such by many, but Marty and I knew he had something fine in him to the point of securing our admiration. It was not a forgone conclusion though, after all.

ABENDA: Oh! So what else happened?

NOBOLA: Marty told me she still needed a clergyman's stamp of approval before unshakingly settling for the adoption of the problematic name. We then paid a visit to the local priest at the Catholic church of Magaville two weeks after Ivy's birth for her to be blessed.

Nobola could remember, despite their spontaneous agreement to give a nice name to their child, Marty repeatedly telling him that they needed to pay a visit to the priest. They secured an appointment, and on a Tuesday afternoon two weeks following Ivy's birth, they met Father Gilbert.

MARTY: Hello, Father Gilbert! We have come so you can bless our newborn baby.

FATHER GILBERT: You are welcome to the house of the Lord, my children! May God be with you all, always.

Amen.

Father Gilbert was known to Nobola and his family from a long time. He happened to be the one parishioner baptizing all three of their other kids. He used to hold all religious ceremonies that Nobola and his wife considered essential for the family. Father Gilbert, for that reason, used to be dearly referred to as "the father of the family" by them.

FATHER GILBERT: What's the child's name?

MARTY: Ivy.

FATHER GILBERT: Oh, good! Now, did you first verify if the name is canonized?

MARTY: No, Father.

FATHER GILBERT: Well, that does not really matter to God because, after all, he always welcomes every baby in the world with his grace and mercy, and his doors are always open to each one of us, his sons and daughters, no matter where we come from. We all live thanks to his clemency and misericord; he loves us no matter what name we carry.

NOBOLA: But, Father, many say that those who inspired us to our daughter's name are sinners.

FATHER G.: Behold my son, because "all have sinned," says the Lord! If someone did you wrong, go and pardon that person, just as Jesus Christ asks us to pardon one another and to live in peace with everyone. My children, in truth, we all are sinners.

The priest, after saying those words, took the little girl in his hands and rose her above his eyes. The two parents were looking up in a silent and grave contemplation as he continued: "I now bless Ivy in the name of the Father and the Son and the Holy Ghost. May the spirit of the Lord be upon you all always, in this life and in eternity!"

"Amen!" they answered in unison. He handed them the baby back and said, "Now is time to go home. Go with the peace of the Lord!" while, with his right hand, making a sign of the cross in the air.

"We are rendering grace to God," they responded and headed toward the parish exit.

Marty and Nobola were relieved and felt reassured when they left the parish. And now Nobola was feeling really happy as he talked about the little trip to his friends.

NOBOLA: After that first couple of weeks doubting, stressing, and almost depressing about our own child's name, we could now walk proudly with the priest's approval as our first line of defense against bullies. The next day, we went to the mayor's office for the birth certificate.

ABENDA: You said you felt as if your baby joy was being stolen!

NOBOLA: Literally! At this point, I had to surrender to the reality that I was surrounded by people who didn't want to see us celebrate. I particularly was being pushed to walk in shame of my own little girl by people who unequivocally told me I had made a mistake by choosing "a wrong name." Their views were those shared by many at the time, that Potus—or anything related to him—was no reason to rejoice. In this I had my dose of pills to swallow. Have you guys noticed such things around you in most recent times?

ASSO: Oh yeah, definitely! It's like an obscure opposition, a dark movement aiming to ensure or convince us that everything the president touches is stained in dirt. Whatever good idea he brings out or good action he accomplishes is downplayed, distorted, or simply ignored. On the other hand, whatever goes wrong is always blamed on him. How fair is that? Is he not an American like the rest of us?

NOBOLA: This is how such people connect to the extremist politicians of the left. Together they form a curiously dark, or I should say blue-looking, portion of the country, one with people fed with and regurgitating obscurantist patterns of behavior. They consider individually achieved socioeconomic progresses an abnormality and individual efforts for enterprenial success a sin. Because Potus will always defend that side of free enterprise in America, they hate him as a result. Instead, they like to encourage people who want to forever depend on social-assistance programs from the government, because that's the best way to run dictatorships.

EKIEY: I hear you, John, and I am telling you this: the Dems and others on the left use these tactics with one goal in mind: to create an American reality the likes of which we have not seen before in this country. The culture that derives from that reality is one of self-doubts, sorrow-emulating disgust for economic progress and those who thrive for it.

NOBOLA: Exactly! This totally and accurately describes the kind of world most Dems and their Communist allies want us to live in. The consequences thereof are unintended sometimes and more often well engineered, those of Americans becoming ashamed of themselves, of their honest efforts, and curiously, of their flag. This is shameful, indeed. It is painful! This is not what many like me came to see. America is better! America deserves better!

CHAPTER 8

Mars Vegas

On Mars Day that year, Nobola, Abenda, and two other friends were on a trip to celebrate the occasion in Mars Vegas, a special town situated in the Nevada desert and in close proximity with Las Vegas, the iconic city. Named after the SpaceX Mars 20 Mars human colonial program, Mars Vegas is made of a series of big tent-style housing bubbles mixed in varieties of vegetal species and enclosed in a bigger bubble from much thinner and transparent material the size of a big city.

The town builders' idea was to replicate the environment within the American Mars colony, and in order to accomplish this, they figured an ecosystem where the ambient atmosphere is completely separated from natural earth conditions. Though Mars Vegans live with the same air as Mother Earth, that air is simply filtered through the bubbles, freed from all common pollutants. Sun rays are filtered as well, and the town is never touched by natural rainwaters ●.

Life within Mars Vegas goes like anywhere else in America. The exception is no inhabitant stays there more than two weeks at a time, but babies who born there are kept within the boundaries of the bubble until they reach the age of eighteen; then they can choose to move to Mars or Mother Earth, or simply remain the sole permanent residents of the special city.

There are many attractions in Mars Vegas, with one of the best being the Martian life museum. The museum is, unlike most other bubble buildings, pyramidal in shape, with the summit pointing up beyond the big bubble's top. People say that the summit is how Earthians make direct contact with their Martian counterparts.

Access to the town is open to all on a "first come, first serve" basis and according to availability of living slots determined based on the town's one hundred thousand people capacity. No weapons are allowed but for the National Army, whose protective personnel are actually kept outside the bigger bubble, guarding the entire surrounding areas.

Mars Day was especially dedicated to the public policy personnel, a.k.a. PPP. On this day, PPPs from all parties meet in Mars Vegas along with their unaffiliated colleagues for joint extra business activities, and the day is considered the best bet for the US president to be present. This year, Potus was there playing in the same team as Déjà vu, his Democrat challenger, as the PPPs staged a football game against the National Army team.

Nobola and friends had secured an admission to the bubble too and were having dinner inside a McDonald's. Solong Zolo, one of them, was always of the forthcoming type.

SOLONG: John, people are talking about your interventions at the forum. I hear they have them all over the podcasts and other social media, and I think it's all BS.

NOBOLA: Did you even take the time to listen or read?

SOLONG: I don't take any crap from Reps, so I didn't even bother to listen.

NOBOLA: Well, how then do you decide that it's BS if you didn't check the content of my exposes?

SOLONG: I just told you, I am a Democrat, like Mom and Dad, Uncle Paul, your wife Marty's dad, is a Dem too. But these days, I hear Marty say she's followed you in becoming a Rep. I wonder what is going on with both of you. To vote Democrat runs in the family!

NOBOLA: We choose to be Reps because we think embracing a political stand doesn't have to be conditioned solely based on family culture. Political participation is more important than that, so we defend an agenda that we know is going to serve our vision of life.

SOLONG: And what is this vision, my brother?

NOBOLA: The Republican message to the people is consistent with the truth about everyday life. We present and tackle reality the way it is. We know society has highs and lows; we don't pretend to run or create a perfect world. Therefore, if we fail, we fail together; and in success, we ride with everyone. That's the way Potus's economic prowess has united the people.

You Dems instead, you always have a nice and beautiful discourse, filled with promises of a society that is impossible to achieve except by imposing your views on what it's got to be, though contrary to the path that leads everyone to happiness and freedom.

SOLONG: What we want is equality!

NOBOLA: I know! Dems pretend to achieve equality for all even by ways of breaking the law. That does not serve peace and order. It only serves to consolidate their leadership power at the expense of the people's freedom. This power, which many prominent Democrats have vowed to carry around the world, recruiting accomplices in demagogic foreign leaders to forge a lunatic globalist order, and this while using the American taxpayer's money, sometimes against their own will or interests. This power they are using to teach society delusion, lies, demagogy, not dignity, integrity, reality, and honor, the cardinal values that guided the foundation of this great nation.

Abenda and Simpla, their other friend, had been watching Nobola and Zolo debate with a decent amount of interest. Then they noticed that the discussion was nowhere near a close.

SIMPLA: You both will go on for hours of debating Potus! Come on.

ABENDA: Oh yeah, fellas, enough of Potus now! Does anyone know why the PPPs are the only ones to have a special day here?

SIMPLA: Yes. Most of these folks don't have enough time to come here otherwise. They have a tough mandate of working for We the People (WTP) and are on a compelling schedule as a result.

ABENDA: Well, their presence here is seriously advertised!

SIMPLA: True. They are always newsworthy; that's politics. It gets people the spotlight.

SIMPLA: I think it is more of an honor, mutual, both for the PPPs and the WTPs, to witness or experience this day every year. The PPPs get immersed in the lifestyle of average Americans, and the WTPs get a chance to see the PPPs under same circumstances as the rest of us.

ABENDA: I think they are all brothers and sisters. They simply have a duty to work for us every day, speaking for our common differences in a context that often puts them into antagonistic opposition to each other. Mars Day can always shed all doubts about their brotherhood. Is that not an example for us?

NOBOLA: It is! The whole Mars Vegas experience allows us to see ourselves on a shared quest, one of a future where we find comfort in looking beyond our dissents. That's when we reset the button on the ways of our lives as we face bigger challenges, so we live for what we all cherish most: promise of freedom. We must always remember that in God we trust, and each time we come together, we must recover all that "in mobs, we lost.

There was a sudden silence around the dinner table. Everyone was listening, and for a good moment, heads kept nodding in agreement.

SOLONG: Hey, John, I still want to go back to our talk earlier and tell you how much I appreciate your motivation, man! Potus's momentum must be giving you wings, I think. What will you do when he's no longer in power? You probably will go back to being them, a Dem again, right?

NOBOLA: Nope, Solong, never! As I told you earlier, pursuit of the winning label is not what I hold civic participation to be about. We Reps like Potus because he is a great leader, but most importantly, he inspires us with his sense of commitment to serve our country beyond and sometimes against partisan protocols. He will leave the office one day, but his exemplary stand for the defense of real America will carry on. His example will remain a precious tool for the people to use in order to check and balance the blind power grab by a faction, be it Democrat or another.

Index

7-Eleven, 42

A

Abenda, Isaac, 1–3, 10, 13, 16, 25–26, 30–31, 38, 41–42, 48, 64, 73, 77
abused laborers, 60
Africa, 18, 62
allegiance, 56
America, 4, 8, 13, 22–23, 32–36, 40–43, 45–48, 50–51, 56, 61–62, 72, 74
American Constitution, 60
American culture, 34, 37, 48–49
American dream, 5, 24, 32, 35, 41, 62
American flag, 14, 47, 56
American Mars, 73
Americans, 13, 41–44, 54, 60, 72, 77
American society, 2, 7, 40
American values, 14, 21
anarchist groups, 2
anarchists, 35, 39, 50, 59–60
Asso (colleague), 63–64
Ayatollah, 5

B

Badenoch, Kemi, 39
Bamotoland government, 62
Benson (Jamaican friend), 25
black electorate, 4–5
black people, 1–3, 5–6, 17, 40, 46, 57
BNN, 19

C

capitalism, 51–52
chaos, 45, 47
China, 44, 51, 53
citizens, 18, 36, 49, 51, 53
civility, 43, 47
colonists, 38, 60
Communism, 40, 51–52, 60
Communists, 48, 51
communities, 2, 17, 50
  black, 5, 50
  tribal, 56
Constitution, 40–42, 60
constitutional rights, 49

Lightning Source UK Ltd.
Milton Keynes UK
UKHW041937150321
380411UK00009B/1137/J